Words for Weary Wanderers

By Victoria Grace

Copyright Information

Words for Weary Wanderers

Cover: Madeline Gehman

ISBN: 979-8-218-48363-0

Early Reviews

"*Words for Weary Wanderers* felt like having a bird's eye view into the author's personal journals. The poems and short stories beautifully conveyed the raw emotional experience of chronic pain, depression, and the healing power of nature and poetry. There's community and connection in the words. And the author's description of her experiences in nature makes me want to don a backpack and head to the Colorado the author so lovingly describes. Among my favorite poems are: *Is There Room For You?, I'm Fine, Falling, Full-Time Job, Wildflower Symphony, Find Me In The Forest,* and *Stones or Flowers: A Short Story*. This book will feel like a gentle hand of comfort and empathy on the shoulders of those who have similar struggles." -Cheryl

"My favorite thing about Victoria's poetry book Words for Weary Wanderers is how clear it is. I've read poetry books where I can't understand the language and it goes right over my head. Upon reading this book I found myself finishing reading one poem and craving for the next one and saying over and over again I can relate to this poem and that poem. I felt so understood. Victoria gave words to thoughts and experiences I have had and learning lessons I never wrote down. I feel like she is a soul sister. Her poetry is so powerful and it just makes sense to me. Victoria is my new favorite poet! You must read this book! It's truly phenomenal and has what it takes to be a bestseller in my eyes!"
-Alexandra

Dedication

For all my fellow weary wanderers, trekking through the woods, seeking relief from their pain through the beauty and hope found in nature.

For those struggling with chronic illness and longing to know they are seen and not alone.

For my husband Eric – my favorite outdoor adventure partner and the guy who reads my writing first and always encourages my passions.

For my readers, to whom I am forever grateful.

Note to Readers

This book is divided into two sections. The first, entitled "Weary and Wondering," explores the authentic and difficult realities of living with chronic illness and mental health struggles. Chronic illness affects every aspect of a person's life. This is why if you come across a poem in the first section about which you think "well, this doesn't seem to be related," the truth of the matter is: it is related. My chronic pain/illnesses affect my personal life, my mental health, my spiritual life, my love life, my friendships, my work, and whether I like it or not, they have impacted who I am as a person and how I relate with the world.

The second section, entitled "Wandering and Words" showcases the beauty and hope I have found as I've wandered through nature and utilized writing as a way to heal.

I have always been drawn to nature. I feel most at home in the woods. I would spend forever in the mountains if I could. The most peace I have ever felt has been beside a bubbling creek. The most joy I have ever experienced has been when the sun is shining down on me. The forest makes me feel free.

I think, part of why I am so drawn to nature and beauty is because my life has been filled with such pain. I have been diagnosed with multiple chronic illnesses, causing me to be unable to remember a day where I was not in pain. I have also struggled with anxiety and severe depression throughout most of my life. The beauty of nature is healing for me, reminding me that there is hope and good still to be found in this broken and weary world.

Writing has always been an outlet for me, where I could express myself authentically. I used to write for my own eyes only, but then I realized there are people who could benefit from my words, so I began publishing them with the goal of welcoming the weary to experience wonder and receive hope.

If, you, too, find yourself weary from endless wandering in search of relief or hope, and a hand to hold as you traverse this journey, this book is for you.

I hope these poems and short stories will serve as a supportive companion for you.

Trigger Warnings Note:

This book contains poems with themes including mental health, suicidal ideation, chronic pain/illness, and trauma healing. Please be gentle with yourself as you read, particularly if you resonate with any of these themes.

National (U.S.) Suicide/Crisis Lifeline: 988. Call or Text.

SECTION 1:
WEARY & WONDERING

My Words

Can my words
Even be heard?
I scream from the rooftops,
Write 'til my ink stops.
Can my words even be heard?
I whisper in the night
And write by candlelight.
Can my words
Even be heard?
I have so much to say
So many things I pray.
Can my words
Even be heard?
I can no longer be silent;
These pen strokes are violent.
Can my words
Even be heard?

Faking

I've become so good at faking
It begins each morning as I'm awakening:
Smiling as I take your order,
Rushing around as I cook your order.
You wouldn't know by looking at me,
But it's what you don't see:
The exhaustion behind my eyes,
The pain behind the smile that says I'm fine.
The way I move you wouldn't know
That when the work day ends, it's home to bed I go.
I can barely move without crying,
But tomorrow, when I'm back, smiling
You'll never know the horror that was my night –
I keep it all, out of sight.

Depression Looks Like:

A smile on my face all day,
Then at home, buried under these covers, I lay.
Dishes piled high,
Every breath comes out as a sigh.
Texts left on read,
Therapy sessions with too much going unsaid.
I don't know how to explain,
And so, I simply refrain.
I suffer alone,
Too afraid to confide,
Always hoping the darkness will someday subside.
I can't find a way through.
One breath at a time is all I can do.
The world thinks I'm fine;
My kitchen sink and these bedroom sheets –
They know otherwise.
And they draw a line straight from my depression
To my current situation.

Shouts Give Way to Silence

You became angry at her silence,
But what else was she supposed to do
When her loudest shouts
Had gone unanswered.

Stay

If you're struggling, stay.
Sometimes unexpected blessings come your way.
If you're breathing and alive today,
Please believe there is a way
For hope to return
Before you crash and burn.
If you weren't here,
You **would** be missed,
So go make that grocery list
Because tomorrow, you **will** wake,
And you'll probably want a pancake.

Emotions

So many different emotions,
Not enough healing potions.
We spend so much time on worry
And push through feelings in a hurry.
We can barely stay afloat,
But what if slowing down is the anecdote.

When Answers Evade

When answers evade
And you long to rebuild that barricade –
The one that keeps your soul safe from harm and hurt
But also leaves you in a desert,
Void of the love you so desperately crave.
So maybe that barricade –
It won't actually save.
Because you cannot prevent the possibility of pain
Without also preventing the possibility for love to pour down like rain
On all your broken parts,
Breaking through to your worn heart.

You opened my eyes to a whole new world,
One where dreams could unfold.
Imagine what I could do without constant companions, aches and pains.
I could make so many gains.
I'm not asking for much –
Just a small healing touch.
I never meant to need you for long,
But am I so wrong
For wanting to feel like a regular person,
One from whom I no longer have to run.

[controlled substance]

Waiting for the other shoe to drop // except it must be a centipede that's losing shoes //because it's not just one or two // these shoes are dropping like buckets of rain // everywhere and all at once

Clothes That Never Dry

Like clothes that never dry,
So is grief and these endless tears I cry.
Every time they almost dry,
A rainstorm rolls in,
Beginning the process all over again.
My face is tear-stained,
These sobs, unrestrained.
My face turns scarlet,
Like the clothes that fill with water droplets,
Turning color, growing darker.
My face only gets redder.
Salty tears land on my lips,
My emotions are not following the scripts.
I can't stop these tears in time – they fall unprovoked.
And I can't bring the clothes inside before they are soaked.

Pain

Pain every inch of my skin
I'm stretched too thin
Not sure where to begin
The aches worsen in my bones
I see the warning cones
Signaling that more pain is up ahead
I'm hanging on by a thread.

Complexities of Love and Pain

There is an ache in my chest,
A stirring in my breast.
I long for your touch,
Yet I feel like I'm too much.
I fear
That you will leave me here
When you realize all my imperfections;
My heart may not be able to handle more rejections.
I find it safer to retreat within this shell,
But what if I could rebel
Against these fears that hold me hostage,
Keeping me in bondage.
What if I could find love and healing,
Even as I'm still reeling
From the hurts that wounded so deeply.
I long to live and love freely.

Covers Thrown Back

Covers thrown back,
Like you left with the intention of coming right back.
But you never did.
And I never fixed the bed.
I left them rumpled, instead
Because it hurts too much
To think of never again feeling your touch.

Boundaries

I mark the spot // with a stake // driven in only halfway // I know that I ought // to make these boundaries stick // but I am afraid // and maybe I'd rather be burned // like the end of a candle wick // I know it doesn't make sense // but I am addicted to chaos // and if I put up a fence // I might actually find peace from the mess

Cut Down

You cut her down as if she were a dead tree. And then you burned her passions and hopes, as if they were logs.

Through the Fog

Through the fog,
Though my vision's blurred,
I reach for you.
I won't be deterred.
Same is true of my healing;
I can't see what's ahead,
But I will continue
To put one foot in front of the other
Until the fog clears
And I see
That, all along,
I was moving forward.
Moving toward healing.

Exhaustion

Exhausted.
From trying to stay alive.
To thrive –
I can't even think about thriving,
For simply surviving
Takes every ounce of my will
And even still –
There is almost not enough energy,
For it takes so much synergy
Between my body and mind.
I fight to be kind.
For I know that this body has been through so much trauma,
Can't deal with any drama,
She's just trying to stay alive.
Maybe someday, she will thrive.

From the Perspective of My Hospital Bed:

I welcome your weary, pain-wracked body.
I can feel your anxiety as you sink into me.
I can sense your fears, your doubts;
You wonder if today will make a difference.
So many promises made by the healthcare system,
But only leaving you more broken,
Trust shattered.
I wish that I could transfer some of your burdens onto myself, but,
I, too, am weary
From holding up all of these broken bodies over the years.
I wish that I could speak,
Tell you that you're not alone.
I've held so many before you,
With similar questions, doubts, and fears,
Similar pain and exhaustion.
After hours of waiting, poking, and prodding,
You go limp, and I can tell that you're finally out,
Sleeping peacefully, I hope.
They wheel us back to the surgery room.
I carry you, and silently, I pray.
That they will not let you down,
That you might be one I never see again.
Not because I don't care for you.
But because, you're healed.
And don't need to return to this place –
This place of pain and fear.
I am stuck here.
This is my job, what I was made to do.
Sometimes I wonder why I could not have been a different kind of bed,
Perhaps a comfortable king-size, holding space for rest and

pleasure,
Instead of pain.
But if I am being honest,
I would not have it any other way.
For perhaps, I can bring comfort.
And that is my purpose, as a hospital bed.
But still, I sink
And feel myself wearying.

Finally Rest

I sink into the bed
Pull the covers up
I can finally rest my head
And allow to overflow, the cup
Of feelings and pain
That I keep hidden
While trying to stay sane
Until the emotions bubble up, unbidden.
For, after all, I am only human.

Friendships Lost

If they never reach out first,
If they can't handle you at your worst,
If they only get together with you as a last resort,
If they no longer feel like a support,
If they cancel on you when something "better" presents,
Yet they still want to offer their two cents,
Perhaps they aren't the friend you thought
And true friendship can't be bought.
Perhaps you must let go,
Though it hurts so.

Is There Room for You

What if your heart hurts
And your soul can't sing?
Is there still a place for you?
What if you have not yet found beauty in the broken?
What if acceptance has yet to replace anger?
Is there still room for you here?
What if all you feel is emptiness?
And joy escapes you?
Is there a safe haven for you?

Pain Is: (a list poem)

-every hour, every moment, for as long as I can remember
-both internal and external
-unwanted company
-an intruder
-one who refuses to leave
-squeezing its talons into every inch of my body
-curled up on the floor, begging and pleading for relief
-canceled plans on a Friday night
-in bed by 8:00pm on a Saturday night
-sleepless nights, tossing and turning, never able to get comfortable
-heating pads in every room
-a concoction of meds so large I may as well be the pharmacist myself
-loneliness
-feeling misunderstood
-uninvited, forgotten
-doubled over, so intense I think I may pass out
-hoping I don't wreck the car
-just praying I can make it through the work day
-feeling betrayed by my own body
-questioning my very existence
-wanting to die
-also needing to prove my strength
-exhausting
-never-ending, with no end in sight
-my reality.

Glimmer

I ask for a glimmer of hope;
I receive only a shiver,
Signaling things will only grow colder, not warmer.
But I am already so frigid;
If it gets any worse, I might not make it.
I’ve cried and I’ve begged and I’ve pleaded
But none of my efforts have succeeded...

I ask for some alone time but then the whole time all I do is worry something bad happened to you. My mind conjures up a hundred different disastrous scenarios.

[anxiety]

Please Stay

Please stay.
There are still people left to love,
More struggles to rise above.
This is merely a chapter,
You need to find out what comes after.
Perhaps there is harmony to your melody,
Perhaps it is possible to live free.
This chapter of your story could serve as a guide
In a way it wouldn't if you'd died.
Please stay.

I'm Fine

Behind my smile
Lie years of copy pasted replies:
"I'm fine," while forcing my lips to curve upwards.
Meanwhile, with each fake smile,
These lips crack a little more
Until it hurts too much to force the smile.

Burnout

Burnout is like the end of the ketchup bottle where you know there's a little bit left and you're just trying to squeeze it out before calling it quits.

Change

"But they're all good changes," they protest.
But can't good changes still create stress?
Just because it's good doesn't mean there are no mixed emotions
About the fact that nothing will remain –
Or ever again be – the same.

Where I Fit

I worry I won't fit.
That things will shift.
So much so that, for me, there won't be a place.
Just an empty space.
Where I used to sit.
Before I no longer fit.

Can't Find the Light

I know it's not right
And yet it feels like all I have left.
It's all so heavy
And I can't find the light,
So I dance drunkenly by night,
Hoping to awake to a brighter day.

Medicine Caps

Dang child locks
On medicine caps
Preventing chronically ill me
From getting the bottle open
For even a little relief
From this pain that debilitates.
Throwing the bottle across the room,
Cursing,
Then sobbing,
Because I feel so weak
And I can't get even a little relief.

Anger

Talons in my chest,
Fire in my breath,
The anger overtakes me,
Grasping for someone or something to release
All this pent-up rage
That I've carried for ages.

Kindling

You tossed me into the fire as if I was kindling. And then you watched me. Slowly, slowly burn. Until all that was left were the ashes of who I used to be.

Slab of Wood: a short story

I feel like a slab of wood, being mutilated by a carpenter who never should have been allowed to do that trade. He shoves in the nails, then twists them around, pounds with the hammer – a few extra swings, more than necessary – whatever causes the most pain and the least gain. When he's finally finished, he realizes I'm not what he had imagined after all. So, he shoves me away, into an old closet. Forgotten. Surrounded by darkness.

But at least, maybe here, I won't hurt so bad. The darkness crushes me, and I feel trapped. But somehow, I learn to function here: finally settling into a routine, finding hope in the slits of light that seep through the cracks in the door.

Until one day, he comes back. He says he is going to fix me up. Perhaps, there is hope.

Until he begins sawing and banging. This time, even worse than the last. And I'd rather he left me alone in that cramped, dark closet.

Surely that, would be better than this. I beg to go back, to return to that closet – for at least, I had learned how to manage that darkness. This new darkness is simply too much. I can't do this again, I plead. But he won't let me go. Almost as though he enjoys torturing me so.

So you see, this is how I came to believe that the very one who created me, also hates me.

Hiding in the Shadows

Hiding in the shadows,
Dodging the light,
Walking circles around the neighborhood,
My pup, stopping often to sniff,
Oblivious
To the tears falling down my face.
Out here, at least,
I feel the comfort of nature and nighttime
Versus the four suffocating walls, tossed pillows, and body wracked with sobs.
On nighttime walks, my tears become a part of nature,
Watering the flowers.
I like to think they help the flowers grow,
Just as they contribute to my growth and healing, too.

Lying on the Bathroom Floor

Lying on the bathroom floor,
Praying to make it to the door.
Gripping the steering wheel,
Tears streaming down my face.
It all seems so surreal,
And yet somehow also de ja vu.

I've been here before.
And I've begged, "Please, no more."
Getting up feels like such a chore,
Every bone in my body is so dang sore.

I long for purpose in the pain,
But it seems there is simply nothing to gain.
It's making me go insane.

My only hope is that I can encourage another,
Who is also lying on the bathroom floor,
Praying to make it to the door.

Falling

I'm falling. But I'm so good at faking it that you think I'm still climbing. But my harness was never even attached. I'm falling.

Words Won't Come

Lately, words won't come.
Don't know what I'm running from.
Or maybe, this is the pain of heading towards
Healing and moving forward.
Maybe, through the breaking,
I'll find whatever it is I'm craving.
Maybe, I'm running from darkness
And toward hope and its fullness.
Maybe I am no longer running from the past
But toward something that will last.

Full-time Job

Pretending I'm fine when I'm actually falling apart and faking I'm okay when the pain is actually unbearable is a full-time job. A job that I excel at. With twenty plus years' experience, I should add it to my resumé.

Scars

Our scars – we try to hide them
Our scars – we believe they are ugly.
But my scars – they tell a story.
Of a girl who overcame.
My scars – they tell a story.
Of a girl who experienced deep pain.
My scars – they tell a story.
Of a girl who experienced grace and growth.
My scars – they are a reminder.
Of all that I have overcome.
My scars – they are a message.
For others needing to know they don't have to be ashamed of their scars.
My scars – they ache sometimes.
But my scars – they made me who I am.

Weather

Life is often like the Colorado weather. One moment, sunny. The next, with no warning, snow blizzards all around. One moment, you're hope-filled and happy. The next, your entire world comes crumbling down. No warnings. But what if we had warning? Would we prepare? Or would it keep us from getting out and enjoying the clear-sky moments?

Hit the Brakes

For goodness sakes,
Slow down, hit the brakes.
Can't believe you're still awake,
Even with all that is at stake –
[By "all" I mean your health, your sanity,
The healing of sorrows from which you flee].
If only you could see what I can see:
That you are worth caring for, and it's okay to simply be.

Worn Out from Being a Burden

My throat is raw from screaming,
My knees are sore from praying,
My fingers ache from reaching for answers,
My feet are battered from the traverse,
My eyes are tired from longing,
My ears tingle from listening,
My heart is discouraged
From searching for answers to questions that seem only to be a burden.

Postponed

The train has derailed,
The ship has already sailed.
My opportunity, my fresh start –
It's gone, like ships out at sea, like dandelions in the wind.
But ships return; scattered dandelions plant new seeds.
Perhaps my fresh start has simply been postponed.
Perhaps it isn't gone, but simply looks different than I'd planned.

My Demons

I went dancing with my demons,
Showed them all sorts of freedoms,
Freedoms I could experience if they weren't dragging me down.
We danced and sang out loud,
Then slow-danced without a sound.
Until we came to a mutual understanding:
I'm sick of pretending.
I want to dance freely.
And they've already taken enough of me.

Dreams

Once upon a daydream...
Dreams so big I could soar...
But I don't dream anymore.
Can we go back to the way it was before?
When I dreamed so big it sounded improbable,
Maybe even impossible,
And yet I fully believed it was doable,
That the dreams were achievable.

Storm

Caught in the storm,
Buckets of rain pouring down,
Lightning strikes all around,
I've not yet found
Beneath this solid ground
A place where shelter could be found.

I run for cover,
Under the wetness, I shiver.
Hair standing up, I quiver,
As the electricity comes nearer,
Will I be struck by lightning, I wonder,
Will I be washed upriver,
Before I have the chance to tell her: I forgive her.

Dormant or Growing

For months, they sit. Seemingly dormant.
I wonder: do the perennials wonder if maybe they've died, never to return to the gardens they have grown to love?
I wonder: do they get discouraged, ponder giving up and giving in?
Until.
A tiny bud of hope appears,
Only for them to fret over its growth being too slow.
Suddenly, one day, there is a full-blown gorgeous flower.
And we are shocked.
How did this happen?
While we thought nothing was happening,
It was growing all along -
But beneath the surface.
Unseen.
But growing, nonetheless.

SECTION 2:
WANDERING & WORDS

Wildflower Symphony

A wildflower symphony
Drowning out the cacophony,
So many voices telling me how I should be,
But I prefer to be free.
Like wildflowers that grow wherever they please,
I no longer wish to appease.
There is beauty in chaos,
But in conformity, I feel lost.
I'm learning to be like a wildflower,
Living free.

When I Feel Chaos in My Soul

When I feel chaos in my soul,
When the pain of this world takes its toll,
I go on a hike or get on a kayak and float;
Nature and beauty are the anecdote.
The solution to darkness is light;
The way to find freedom is by taking flight.
Travel the forests, the streams,
Chase the sunbeams.
Forge new paths,
And you'll find a healing salve.
Leave the screens
For new routines.
Dance in the rain –
It just may keep you sane.
Seek out childlike wonder,
And never give up the adventure for which you hunger.

Stress Dies Here

Water is toxic to stress –
It could never survive on the lake –
For the lake doesn't seek to impress,
Or fret over all the mistakes it could make.
The lake only supports peace and life;
There is no space for strife.
It flows steadily and freely,
Relishing in creating calm and beauty.

Meaningless fragments of memory float around my mind
No pieces to connect them that I can find –
The lake soothes.

Shattered pieces of happiness,
The lies telling me I am worthless –
The lake heals.

Worries over things not yet,
Heavy burdens with no place to set –
The lake carries them.

Aching bones,
Body full of stones –
The lake offers rest.

Water heals,
For stress dies here.
With each gentle ripple of waves,
A life is saved.

Embracing the Slower Pace

Learning to embrace
A slower pace:
The tortoise and the cheetah both have their place.
We can miss so much when we do everything with such haste:
Copy and paste,
Erase and replace.
But what if we took a break,
What if rest isn’t a waste,
What if, for this too, there is grace?

Under the Vast Colorado Sky

Under the vast Colorado sky,
I feel so light and free, like a bird I could fly.
Fly far, far away and stay,
Until sorrows and stresses wash away,
Until peace floods my soul,
And I feel whole.

Nature Therapy

Nature therapy
Is what it's called
When you allow the woodland critters
To hear your sorrows
And the bubbling brook
To carry them all away.

Find Me in the Forest

I'm not trying to be a tourist;
You can find me in the forest.
I don't need a florist
When I have wildflowers all around.
Canopies of green surround.
Bubbling creek and chirping birds the only sound.
Beauty in every corner of the woods is found –
A perfect view.
I'm a mountain woman, through and through.

Life I Was Made For

When the gray of these walls is all I can see,
The weight of this world crushes me.
No longer willing to pay that price,
The woods became my paradise.
The only high I chase
Is the feeling of warm sun on my face.
I'm addicted to the peace that comes from floating on a lake.
Each weekend, these moments I embrace.
And all week long, I dream
Of the next time I get to walk alongside a stream.
Spending time outdoors has never felt like a chore –
This is the life I was made for.

300-Year-Old Trees

Today, I felt small,
Surrounded by 300-year-old trees,
Still standing tall.
I felt small.
They tower above, reaching towards the sun,
Shining through, creating a canopy of leaves and light,
For all the woodland critters and weary wanderers – like me.
I feel small beneath their majesty,
But this is okay.
For I am reminded this world is so much bigger than my one little corner of it.
When I need a reminder,
I will return to these trees –
For they continue to stand tall
When I feel small.

A Place of Safety

A place of safety,
The woodland creates –
A canopy of stars,
Accompanying her scars.
Towering trees,
Carrying her worries away with the breeze.
Bubbling brook,
Washing away tears she cries over all that others took.
Changing leaves,
Providing hope for she who grieves.
Budding laurel,
Reminding of beauty in a world so often filled with quarrel.
The woodland creates –
A place of safety.

Fire

The fire mesmerized
As I re-energized.
By the fireside
I can confide
All of my worst fears
Over a few beers.
As I watch the flames dancing,
My dreams begin expanding.
As the fire crackles,
A wave of sadness passes.
I am flooded with calm,
These flickering embers, a healing balm.

Snow Globe

It felt like we were standing in the middle of a giant snow globe // the porch lights became a strobe // illuminating each snow flake // I want to bottle them up // as a keepsake // commemorating the calm in the midst of the storm // a reminder of a moment where hope was born // awakening to a fresh blanket of snowy beauty // lessens my distress // it feels like a gift // in the midst of grief // even if it's only brief // in this winter wonderland // snow's magic I finally understand.

Lying on the Forest Floor

Lying on the forest floor,
Looking for an open door,
I peer through canopies of green
And see a sky of citrine.
I dream
Of a life filled with light.
One where we can take flight –
Not in the sense of running from,
But flying freely toward, to the beat of our own drum.

Learning from Nature

Logs crackle and burn,
Words rise up,
As I learn
From the fern.

Up against a sturdy oak, I lean
And from her, I glean
New wisdom, previously unseen.

Springtime is when the world rises from the tomb
And begins to bloom,
Reminding us, through the gloom,
It will be our time soon.

Daffodils, wildflowers, laurel –
They don't quarrel
Over who grows first or faster.
Time will tell;
Each in its own season – all will be well.

There is so much nature has to show;
We simply must be willing to go slow,
To look, listen, learn, and grow.

If You Want to Find Me

If you want to find me,
Go to the mountains,
Go to the forests,
Run your hands across the 300-year-old bark,
Listen as water laps against the kayak,
Dig your feet into the cool dirt,
Stand amazed at the foot of a towering tree,
Notice the brilliance of color after a rainfall –
In these places, you will find me,
For I have left a piece of my heart all over these mountains,
across the lakes, and through the woods.

If It Weren't for the Woods

If the woods had not shown me, I would not know joy.

If the sun had not shown me how it continued to rise each new morning, I would not know what it means to shine – and to rise, after the night.

If the trees had not shown me, I would not know how to persevere and keep growing, reaching for light.

If the wildflowers had not shown me, I would not know how to be wild and free.

If the miles of mountain laurel had not shown me, I would not know beauty.

If the bubbling brooks had not shown me, I would not know how to find calm and take deep breaths.

If the woodland critters had not shown me, I would not know when to fight and when to hunker down.

If the bears had not shown me, I would not know how to care for my "cubs," to love, and protect.

If the leaves had not shown me the way they change with the seasons, I would not know that I'll be okay in changing seasons, too.

If the lakes had not shown me, I would not know peace.

If the oceans had not shown me, I would not know courage, through the waves – the ups and downs – of this world.

If the mountains had not shown me, I would not know how high I could go.

If the valleys had not shown me, I would not know that it is possible to get through them.

If the turtle had not shown me, I would not know how to slow down.

If the storms had not shown me, I would not know that it is possible to survive them.

If the butterflies had not shown me, I would not know there is beauty after the cocoon and that coming out of our comfort zones can be beautiful.

If the night had not shown me, I would not know how healing it is to lie under the stars.

If the dark had not shown me, I would not know how to appreciate the light of day.

If the forest did not exist, I would not be who I am today,

For nearly all that I have learned, the woods have taught me.

Breathe It In

Breathe it in –
Winter has passed.
At last.
Spring is in the air.
Calming hues of blues,
Cheery shades of bright and happy,
Vibrant greens, reminders of life.
Nature becomes fully alive, bringing new life to my soul.
Breathing in deeply and exhaling slowly,
Along with the cool, calm breeze,
I believe.
I can become fully alive again, too.

Nature Healing

Slip off those sandals,
Let the feel of the grass between your toes ground you.
Savor the sunshine.
Believe in the beauty.
Listen to the lake,
Revel in its ripples.
Embrace the environment.

Day of Fun

Mini waves, coming towards, dip after dip.
But try to stop one, and right through your fingers it will slip.
Glistening and rolling, gently;
Calling my soul toward the heavenly.
It amazes me. How it never seems to stop.
Drop after drop.
The oceans, the lakes, the rivers, the creeks,
A splash lands on my cheeks.
I soak in the sun,
Enjoying a day of fun.

Freshly Mowed Grass

The smell of freshly mowed grass
Takes me back
To mudpies and creek walking
To make believe and bike riding
To neighbors who are best friends
To nights you never want to end
To lightning bugs and star gazing
To campouts and water balloon fighting
To simpler times –
A respite from the chaos in my young mind.

Stones or Flowers: A Short Story

Weary and weighted down, a girl with tear-stained face and mud-caked boots trudged down to the river. Upon reaching her favorite spot, she lowered herself onto the biggest rock she could find. She stared, mesmerized, as the creek flowed steadily. This was a facet of nature she would never grow tired of watching. "Oh to be so free," she murmured. To her surprise, she heard a voice reply, "You can be." Startled, she looked all around but saw no one. Again, the voice: "What do you have in that bag you're carrying? It looks very heavy." The girl realized the voice was coming from the water. Was the creek talking to her? She replied, "Honestly, I don't even know what all is in here, but it is heavy." "Take it off." "I...can't," said the girl. "It's been here so long, I don't even know how." Suddenly, a gentle breeze blew through the forest, lifting her bag right off her shoulders. "Open it," the creek instructed. The girl did so, revealing mounds of small stones. Written on each stone was a word. "Read each aloud and then hurl them into my water, one by one," the creek commanded, in a voice that left no room for question. Slowly, the girl picked up the first stone and turned it over. "Shame," she read. "Now throw it in. You don't need to carry that around anymore." The girl hesitated, before gently tossing the stone. She watched it sink, down, down, out of sight. "Now do the next one." "Worthless." "Ugly." "Broken." The girl continued one by one, feeling lighter as she went, until finally – what felt like hours later – the bag was completely empty. "Well done," said the creek. "Now I have something for you." The wind blew again, leaves rustled, and a pile of flowers appeared beside the girl. She picked up a few of them, noticing that, like her rocks, they also had words printed on them. But these words were different. Words such as: "Beautiful." "Beloved." "Worth it." "Brave." "Kind." "Put those in your bag now," the creek instructed. "Many people filled your bag with hurtful words, and you've carried them around for far too long. Allow these new words to remind you who you are. These flowers have special powers, so when you meet someone else whose bag looks heavy like yours once was, someone who looks weighted down by the pain of life, offer them a flower. Each flower can remove the weight equivalent of a few stones. Make the world a lighter, happier place." "Th-thank you," the girl stammered, amazed, as she stood, by how much lighter and free she now felt. The girl could not wait to share some of her newfound "happy flowers," as she took to calling them. On her way back, she met a boy who looked exhausted. He was carrying a water jug and explained that it was for his mother who was dreadfully ill. The girl handed him a flower, which said "Brave." The boy thanked her and continued walking, with a new bounce in his step. The girl smiled and continued in search of the next person with whom she could share another of her flowers. Soon, her entire village would be filled with people who exchanged flowers instead of stones.

What Poetry Means to Me

At a time when no one else was there for me,
Poetry showed up for me.
When no words could leave my lips,
Poetry became my scripts,
My voice in the void,
When I thought all else had been destroyed.
Words filled blank pages,
Thoughts unleashed from their cages.
Poetry became my therapy,
How I processed difficult emotions and feelings
Revealing
The pain, the trauma, the sorrow, the hurt.
It dug up all that dirt.
The dirt that had been buried beneath years of betrayal and disbelief,
All of the grief
Reared its ugly head,
All those words left unsaid –
They finally had a place to land.
Poetry took my hand
And led me to a healing space,
It became my only safe place.
And when there was no one to listen,
Poetry became my friend and let me out of the prison
Of my mind.
I left it all behind.
Poetry
Set me free.

Words as Weapons

Too tiny to hold a sword,
But internally, I roared.
Once too small,
Now, I stand tall.
I could not fight back then,
But I took up a pen.
My words became my weapon,
They are my expression.
And now, I fight for others with my words.
And I write, so they can feel heard.

Words Won't Wait

What can I say,
I write poetry all day.
A thought could come to me anytime, anywhere –
While cutting a cucumber at work,
Driving or hiking,
In the shower,
While washing dishes,
Walking my pup,
In the hospital, awaiting surgery,
At night, while insomnia takes hold.
I have written in all sorts of locations –
In the middle of the woods, back against a log,
Wrapped in a cozy blanket, tears streaming down my face,
On a lake, filled with peace and joy.
In a doctor's office waiting room, anxious and facing
uncertainties, questions without answers.
And perhaps the craziest: along the side of a road
Where I pulled over because so much poetry was bubbling up
while driving, faster than I could possibly write it all down.
But I had to try.
Because words won't wait.
They flow whether it's convenient or not.
And sometimes there is only a window of time.
Before they are lost.
So I must catch them on paper
Before they fly away.
Lost in the clouds.
Never again to be found.

I scribble on napkins, type on a laptop, mostly write in my favorite leather journal –
Whatever I have will do.
Because, like I said, words won't wait.
They won't wait for proper writing instruments.
They won't wait for a convenient time.
Use your own blood, if you must,
Drop everything and write.
Because your words – they won't wait.
They just want, no they need, they demand, to be heard.

I thought I was just processing. I never imagined I was creating poetry to share with the world.

[hidden talent]

Present, but not really.
Physically, I'm here.
Mentally, my mind is elsewhere.
I appear to be taking notes studiously,
But really,
I'm scribbling poetic words onto these cream-colored pages.
Because my inspiration won't wait.
It isn't convenient. I can't control when or where I get inspired.
I just know that I must write it all down.
Before it is gone.

[inspiration]

Find You a Someone

Find you a someone who loves adventure just as much as you do,
Who will gladly spend all day in the outdoors with you.
Find you a someone who has a kind face,
A warm embrace.
Find you a someone who loves your dog like one of their own,
Someone who makes you feel seen and known.
Find you a someone who makes you smile,
Find you a someone you can sit quietly with for awhile.
Find you a someone who celebrates your passions,
Who isn't scared away by your imperfections.
Find you a someone who makes forever
Sound less scary and more like a treasure.

Safe

When you ask how I am // and I feel safe enough to fall apart // to give my realest answer // that's the kind of closeness that I want.

Anchor

Be my anchor, mooring me to shore.
Where I was alone before,
I now have someone to ground me to reality,
Someone to see,
When I'm on the brink of disaster,
Falling faster,
Than I could ever catch myself.
But now, I have help.

Silent Moments

It's in these silent moments // late at night // where I finally get a glimpse // of what peace looks like // I must stay awake // because were I to fall asleep // I would lose these precious moments // I want to linger here for awhile.

Hope

I dream of the day
When hope is here to stay.
When the light doesn't fade
And there are more shallow waters to wade.

I long for a day
Where there is more than one way
To exist and be accepted,
To be authentic, and not neglected.

I hope for the day
Where it will be okay
To feel and to heal,
To be real.

I pray for the day
Where we can lay
It all down
On the ground.

I'll cherish the day
When we won't have to pay
Such a high price
For refusing to live under a guise.

Through the Open Windows

Through the open windows,
The breeze blows echoes,
Of meaningless memories, fragments of fleeting feelings,
Which no longer matter, for I've begun healing.
And the glow of the sun whispers to my mind
That joy is mine to find.

Sunshine Dappled Lemons

Sunshine dappled lemons,
Reminding me of heaven
The golden glow
As rays of sunshine flow
Through my open window at golden hour;
Not all lemons are sour –
Some are merely vessels
For whatever delicacy we create,
Allowing us to see more of the sunshine and less of the ache.
In a world filled with questions,
We seek the sunshine dappled lemons,
Reminding us that answers don't always arrive in the sweet and expected,
But more often, they're found in the sour and rejected.

A Smorgasbord of Berries

On this morning's hike, I found so many different varieties –
Wild huckleberries, wineberries, blackberries –
And I was reminded of the variety among us,
The ways we grow through experiences that are tough,
The thistles and thorns we have each walked through,
To get to the healing,
To get to the berries that taste most refreshing.

Doom and Gloom

I sat down in a room
With doom and gloom.
The room was dark, no light could reach.
Then, I walked down the hall to hope's room.
Their room looked much the same as that of doom and gloom.
Except for one thing: the curtains were open and the light poured in.
It is light that makes the difference.
I went back to doom and gloom and asked why they don't simply open their blinds.
They said, for then the light would shine,
Revealing all the broken parts.
They could not change their hearts,
And they chose to fight
Against the light.
But what I learned is simple: the light is never far;
You must simply leave the door ajar,
Open the blinds,
And let it shine.

This Candle

I bring you this candle;
It's small and barely flickering,
But it is light –
And one small flame can grow
Into a roaring fire.
So, take my flame,
And light your own candle.
Then, give your flame to someone else, too.
And so on, and so forth.
Soon, a million little candle flames
Become a roaring fire.
Once, a mere flicker,
Threatening to burn out,
Now, burning bright,
Showing our resilience to the world.

[Never underestimate your one little candle and the power of community]

Tend Your Garden

Tend to your garden;
Don’t allow your heart to harden.
Be softened
To your own needs;
Plant your own seeds.
Before you can water the flowers from another’s toil,
You must first water your own soil.

A Blessing for a New Month

Here's to more quiet mornings, body movement, tuning in to your emotions. Here's to healing, using words to help your weary soul find wonder. Here's to seeking beauty and joy, even in the moments where it would be so much easier to only see the hard. Here's to filling your cup – both literally with smooth, black coffee – and figuratively, with friends who refresh you and hold hope for you when you've misplaced it, yet again. Here's to more embracing of your creative side. Here's to putting one foot in front of the other, embracing new adventures – both in life and on the trails. Here's to rest and gentleness with your body and soul, as they are oh so weary of the ceaseless pain and longing for answers. Here's to more admiring of sunrises and sunsets. Here's to more pondering and praying in the pines. Here's to celebrating the wins – both big and small, both in your own life and the lives of those you love. Here's to holding tightly the ones you love and cuddling your pets. Here's to good food and good company. Here's to new experiences and prioritizing the ones that make you come alive. Here's to making the world just a little bit better of a place.

First Appeared

The following poem(s) were first published elsewhere, prior to being published in this book:

"From the Perspective of my Hospital Bed" was first published in the magazine entitled *the other side of pain* edited by Shelby Leigh and Cass Chaput, with poems from members of Shelby Leigh's Poetry Club.

"Sunshine Dappled Lemons" was inspired by a prompt from @wildflowerspoetry on Instagram and was shared by that page, after winning that week's contest.

Connect with the Author

Victoria is the author of three poetry books in addition to this one:

-Slow Your Pace, Hope a Little Longer
-Finding Hope in Changing Seasons
-Kisses from Kale

If you'd like to connect with Victoria, you can find her on Instagram and TikTok @writetoreconnect.

To sign up for her newsletter, explore her Etsy shop, book a workshop or event, or find more of her books, you can visit: www.writetoreconnect.com.

Finally, if you've enjoyed this book, Victoria would be immensely grateful if you would leave a rating and review on Amazon, Bookshop, Goodreads, or wherever you buy/review books. Positive reviews make a significant difference in reaching a larger audience and mean so much to independent authors.

About the Author

Victoria resides in Pennsylvania in a cozy log cabin in the woods, with her husband and two beloved dogs. Victoria has her Bachelor of Social Work and has worked in the child welfare field, in addition to working for a nonprofit focused on sexual abuse prevention and support for survivors.

Victoria has published three poetry collections prior to this one. Her first two books include themes of mental health, chronic illness, trauma healing, burnout recovery, nature, and hope. Her third poetry collection focuses on heartwarming and hilarious anecdotes about her rescue dog, Kale.

Through her own experiences with chronic illness and mental health challenges, Victoria is able to write with empathy and authenticity on these challenging topics.

In her spare time, Victoria enjoys spending time outdoors hiking, kayaking, ATVing, or simply admiring nature. When she is not writing, Victoria can often be found with a book in her hands. She also enjoys connecting with friends over a good cup of coffee.

Made in the USA
Middletown, DE
06 September 2024

59841771R00060